This Book Belongs To:

this book has a beautiful collection of drawing patterns that would provide
hours of stress relief through creative express.
Designs range in complexity and detail from beginner to expert level.
©2020

this book has a beautiful collection of drawing patterns that would provide
hours of stress relief through creative express.
Designs range in complexity and detail from beginner to expert level.
©2020

this book has a beautiful collection of drawing patterns that would provide
hours of stress relief through creative express.
Designs range in complexity and detail from beginner to expert level.
©2020

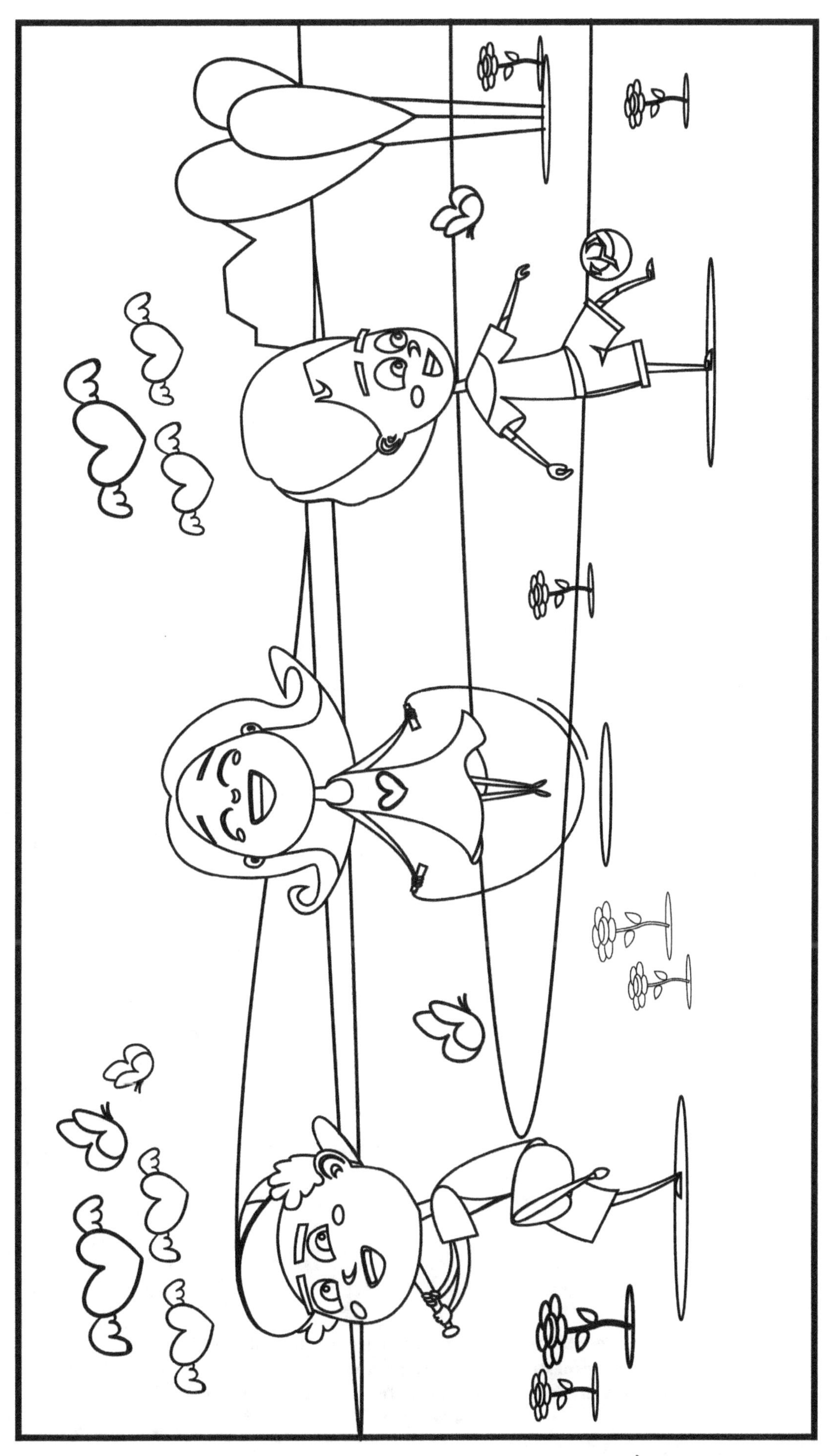

this book has a beautiful collection of drawing patterns that would provide
hours of stress relief through creative express.
Designs range in complexity and detail from beginner to expert level.
©2020

this book has a beautiful collection of drawing patterns that would provide
hours of stress relief through creative express.
Designs range in complexity and detail from beginner to expert level.
©2020

**this book has a beautiful collection of drawing patterns that would provide
hours of stress relief through creative express.
Designs range in complexity and detail from beginner to expert level.
©2020**

this book has a beautiful collection of drawing patterns that would provide
hours of stress relief through creative express.
Designs range in complexity and detail from beginner to expert level.
©2020

SHADOW MATCHING GAMES

this book has a beautiful collection of drawing patterns that would provide
hours of stress relief through creative express.
Designs range in complexity and detail from beginner to expert level.
©2020

this book has a beautiful collection of drawing patterns that would provide
hours of stress relief through creative express.
Designs range in complexity and detail from beginner to expert level.
©2020

Merry christmas

this book has a beautiful collection of drawing patterns that would provide
hours of stress relief through creative express.
Designs range in complexity and detail from beginner to expert level.
©2020

this book has a beautiful collection of drawing patterns that would provide
hours of stress relief through creative express.
Designs range in complexity and detail from beginner to expert level.
©2020

this book has a beautiful collection of drawing patterns that would provide
hours of stress relief through creative express.
Designs range in complexity and detail from beginner to expert level.
©2020

this book has a beautiful collection of drawing patterns that would provide
hours of stress relief through creative express.
Designs range in complexity and detail from beginner to expert level.
©2020

this book has a beautiful collection of drawing patterns that would provide
hours of stress relief through creative express.
Designs range in complexity and detail from beginner to expert level.
©2020

WOOL

this book has a beautiful collection of drawing patterns that would provide
hours of stress relief through creative express.
Designs range in complexity and detail from beginner to expert level.

this book has a beautiful collection of drawing patterns that would provide
hours of stress relief through creative express.
Designs range in complexity and detail from beginner to expert level.
©2020

this book has a beautiful collection of drawing patterns that would provide
hours of stress relief through creative express.
Designs range in complexity and detail from beginner to expert level.
©2020

this book has a beautiful collection of drawing patterns that would provide
hours of stress relief through creative express.
Designs range in complexity and detail from beginner to expert level.
©2020

this book has a beautiful collection of drawing patterns that would provide
hours of stress relief through creative express.
Designs range in complexity and detail from beginner to expert level.
©2020

this book has a beautiful collection of drawing patterns that would provide
hours of stress relief through creative express.
Designs range in complexity and detail from beginner to expert level.

this book has a beautiful collection of drawing patterns that would provide
hours of stress relief through creative express.
Designs range in complexity and detail from beginner to expert level.
©2020

this book has a beautiful collection of drawing patterns that would provide
hours of stress relief through creative express.
Designs range in complexity and detail from beginner to expert level.
©2020

this book has a beautiful collection of drawing patterns that would provide
hours of stress relief through creative express.
Designs range in complexity and detail from beginner to expert level.
©2020

©2020

this book has a beautiful collection of drawing patterns that would provide
hours of stress relief through creative express.
Designs range in complexity and detail from beginner to expert level.
©2020

this book has a beautiful collection of drawing patterns that would provide
hours of stress relief through creative express.
Designs range in complexity and detail from beginner to expert level.
©2020

this book has a beautiful collection of drawing patterns that would provide
hours of stress relief through creative express.
Designs range in complexity and detail from beginner to expert level.
©2020

this book has a beautiful collection of drawing patterns that would provide
hours of stress relief through creative express.
Designs range in complexity and detail from beginner to expert level.
©2020

this book has a beautiful collection of drawing patterns that would provide
hours of stress relief through creative express.
Designs range in complexity and detail from beginner to expert level.
©2020

this book has a beautiful collection of drawing patterns that would provide
hours of stress relief through creative express.
Designs range in complexity and detail from beginner to expert level.

this book has a beautiful collection of drawing patterns that would provide
hours of stress relief through creative express.
Designs range in complexity and detail from beginner to expert level.
©2020

**this book has a beautiful collection of drawing patterns that would provide
hours of stress relief through creative express.
Designs range in complexity and detail from beginner to expert level.
©2020**

This book has a beatiul collection of drawing patterns that would provide
hours of stress relief through creative express .
Designs range complexity and detail from brginner to expert level .
"Designed by brgfx / Freepik"
©2020